Newtown Voices

Sue Cartledge

Newtown Voices

Dedication

Newtown Voices is dedicated to my friend Elizabeth Ban (Liz)
1944–2015, who always believed in my writing ability and
encouraged me to tell these stories as a verse novel;
and to DLC, whose tales of growing up in Marrickville
and Newtown in the 1960s and early 70s led me to fall
in love with the place before I even saw it, and
to hear the language of my characters.

My heartfelt thanks to Mark Tredinnick, who mentored me
through the last eighteen months of the eight-year gestation
of the *Voices*, and without whose advice, tactful edits and
warm encouragement this little book might not exist;
and to my family for all their love and support.

Newtown Voices
ISBN 978 1 76041 341 5
Copyright © Sue Cartledge 2017

First published 2017 by
GINNINDERRA PRESS
PO Box 3461 Port Adelaide 5015
www.ginninderrapress.com.au

Contents

Prologue	7
At the Art Gallery	10
Sunday in the Art Gallery	12
Ultramarine	14
Kalgoorlie; Broken Hill	17
The Graveyard	19
In Croatia	21
An International Village	23
In Brief	26
Damir	27
Scoop!	29
Break-in blackout	32
How I met Harry	33
Mugging Patrols	35
An undercurrent of corruption	36
The Greeks North & South (1)	37
In Newtown	41
Lock the toilets	43
The Yowie	44
Staring at the Upward	46
Bets Raid	49
The Greeks North & South (2)	50
Gambling Terror	52
At the WEA	54
Vice squad acts	56
Sauna mystery	57
Tin Shed Girls	58
The Dream	60
The Subterranean Bar	61
Upstairs at Number 543	63

Gambling clean-up	66
Yellowcake	68
Spag bol and cheesecake	71
Disco dynamo	73
Big boys an small fry	74
Dinner with Harry	76
You can take the girl from Tassie…	78
In Hollis Park	82
I nearly got arrested	83
Dempsey Family wins	85
Cathy's Child	87
Latchkey kids	89
Routine	91
Illegal clubs in full swing	92
At the disco	94
The Greek conspiracy	96
Blacks not wanted	98
After the disco	100
Life wasn't meant to be easy	101
What Tom Doesn't Know	103
Fighting the Yowie	105
Johnny Raper sticks his oar in	107
Pretty poor, Harry, pretty poor	109
In the rain	111
Pushing Rod into the drink	113
David and Damir	116
Back at the Salona Bistro	117

Prologue

King Street, Newtown, September 1977

It's early spring and already hot. The fruit
and veg laid out in boxes at the footpath's
edge are wilting, eggplants sweating
like the cop in his tight serge uniform. A
smallish man of Mediterranean aspect,
the greengrocer's alert, hands behind his
apron, eyes downcast. Jeez, they're all
bloody wogs around ere! Not a local in
sight. The Aussies musta moved out when
all them wogs moved in. Can't say as I

Blame em. Reckon this fella's a dago. Not
as greasy as some of em. Hey you! Jimmy
boy! Mustafa! Move these bloody boxes off
the footpath before someone breaks their leg
on one! Double quick! Shufti! Stupid poofta
doesn't understand a word I'm sayin. Why
can't these wogs speak proper bloody English?
Always jabberin at you, sayin they 'no
unnerstand'. He understands all right. An he'll
understand the weight of me boot if he's not

Too clever. Stupid bastard! Yer can't bloody
put these boxes on the bloody pavement, yer
bloody mug. Never mind 'the fruit she look so
good' an 'the customers they like to see', rubbish.
You no have licence to do that, Mustafa, savvy?
Comprenday? Unnerstand? Now bloody move
them boxes back inside the shop, Jimmy boy,
before I bloody boot yer up the backside an
arrest yer for wastin police time. That put
the wind up the little greaser! Next time I ave

A little chat with im, I might suggest as how
he can get a licence to put them boxes out.
Nice an quiet. Nice an easy. Never let a dago by
without yer fleece em. Squirmy little bastard.
His sister looks a bit of all right but. Jeez,
I wouldn't mind a bit of er, though them wog
kids aint real sheilas. Could put the frighteners
on Mustafa, a cop shaggin is sister. I'll be
keepin me eye on yer, Jimmy boy. Jus you
remember that and don't put them boxes
out onna footpath till I gives yer the say so.

That's the bloody ticket! Dunno why we have
ta put up with all these wogs. Why we let em
inta the country. An their bloody families. I know
its sposed to be cos they'll do all the dirty jobs
we Aussies don't wanna do, but Dad an Uncle
Bill used ta do them jobs, working on the wharves
an mending the roads an that, an Mum an Auntie
Shirl did the sewin at the manchester factory
what these wog and dago bints are doin' now.
That aint bloody right! They're just takin jobs

Away from honest Aussie workers. How can that be
good fer the country like the bloody pollies reckon?
Dirty wogs do them jobs fer less money than what
Dad an Uncle Bill got, and seems them wog bints don't
want as much per sheet or shirt or whatever it is
they sew than what Auntie Shirl an Mum got paid.
They're bloody undercuttin honest Aussie workers.
Where's the bloody unions in all of this, I'd like ta
know? Course we needed em to build the Snowy. Yair,
they was bloody good for that. An maybe fer minin

In the outback, where no sane fella would go
in a fit. But not the bloody city. So yair, some
young fellas to work in the outback or bush, but
why're they allowed to bring their bloody families?
Or worse, marry our sheilas? That aint right! They
should stick to their own kind, an go home to wog
land after they've worked here a coupla years. That
'd be fair enough. More'n they bloody deserve.

At the Art Gallery

Harry

Art Gallery of NSW, Sydney, Sunday, 19 October 1977

I wish I could paint like that. I didn't
know I'd spoken aloud. The man
standing near me, staring hard at
the work as if he could see through
it, mumbling to himself (I thought
he was praying) looked at me, start-
led. Please forgive me, he said, I
did not mean to speak. Courteous.
A bit of an accent. Perhaps European?
I was embarrassed. He'd said some-
thing and thought I'd answered him.
I wish I could paint like that. I'm an
artist. Well, I teach painting. At WEA.
But when I see this – Drysdale – and
the others, Nolan, Blackman, Tucker,
Boyd, Olsen, Margaret Preston – I
know I'll never be an artist, just
a dabbler, a dauber. That's why I
teach. You know the saying, 'those
who can, do; those who can't, teach'?
I was babbling. I'm such an idiot.

This painting is true. Ugly, but true.
He was talking to me, gesturing at
the Drysdale. I have worked in such
places. Not towns but mining camps.
It's harsh, burning at day, freezing
in night. Always empty. Except for
minerals. And giant machines to dig
them out. And towns out nowhere
just some houses, shops, pub. Always
a pub. The pub's the only cool place,
I said, the beer's always cold. Later,
on the way home, I saw him on my
bus. I got off first, so I don't know
where he lives or if we'll meet again.

Sunday in the Art Gallery

Jaroslav

Art Gallery of NSW, Sydney, Sunday, 19 October 1977

I was in the art gallery today, the big
classical building engraved with the
names of famous long-dead artists but
no Old Masters inside, only Australian art.
I like to walk on Sunday mornings. It
feels good to stretch my legs and
breathe free after the trains all week,
and the cheerfully clashing bells of
the cathedral and other churches
remind me a little – not much – of
Sundays in Zagreb. I like to walk
across the Domain – a rough park,
but grass and handsome trees and
birds; some I know – a kookaburra
swings down from a branch to
snatch a worm from the rain-wet
grass then up to perch on a wire
fence; a black bird, his song not
sweet like European blackbirds,
but harsh like schoolboys jeering
at each other 'get real, get real';
little birds scuffling in the leaves.

The gallery is free and open every day and it is cool inside and quiet and I can almost believe I live in a civilised place. But the art confronts me. Such harsh colours. Such ugly shapes. Such emptiness. I am standing in a hot dry place. The burning sun pours at me from the paint – fiery red sky, red ground, red houses. No people. Nothing but scorched sky, earth and empty houses. Yet I recognise this land, if not this town. I have worked in such places. Empty. Unwelcoming. This is my country now, if I truly am New Australian. But the barrenness and heat repels me. I long for green fields and flowing rivers. And birds that sing. Where are the people?

Ultramarine

Harry

King Street, Newtown, Friday, 9 September 1977

Ultramarine! Wrong! Wrong!
It looked right in the sketch but here
on the canvas that broad sweep of blue
just doesn't work. It should swoop
in a dramatic curve from bottom left to
counterbalance the bulk
of that cadmium yellow square top right,
but it's a heavy dreary lunk instead.
How could I have ever thought
that I was an artist?
Oh God, I need a fag!

Back in Lonnie, it was easy. Easy
swanning around as Rod's glamorous wife,
Rod's clever, red-haired (childless) wife
and being 'artistic'. I didn't know
how good I had it then,
until I threw it all overboard –
Rod and Launceston.

Now I'm here, living on my wits
in daggy old Newtown,
some would say slumming it
in ratty, stinking Newtown.
Traffic fumes, roaring trucks and buses,
low-flying planes, beat up cars,
sirens day and night, dogshit
and needles on the footpath.

Not all the smells are bad:
biscuits sweet on the midday breeze
from the factories down the way,
dope from the guy in the building's lee,
warm diesel fumes. But here in the big
smoke my creativity's blown
along with my income.

Look at the traffic crawling paint slow below on King.
Pigeons don't care; up here they rule the roost,
roost on my balcony and every shop's roof.
Go on! Get off, get off, you flying rats!
Fuck this! I need to find some work
or a better way to paint.

But it was fun – a lotus life with Rod
back there when we were first married.
Such a grand society wedding, Lonnie's A-list,
St Andrew's Kirk, reception at Brickenden.
You wouldn't have known
that David was dead
and Toby had shot through to Melbourne.
Lonnie's good at covering up the dirt.

It had to fall apart, I guess,
that easy life. Whatever the surface
the grief's still there, locked in my heart
behind my parents' eyes.
And David's still dead
and Rod's still an arsehole.

Well, I have my life here
and so what if I'm lonely
and angry and broke
and can't paint?
Work! Work's supposed to be good
for what ails you,
my dad always said.
I've got to find work and maybe then
I'll find myself in daggy Newtown.

Kalgoorlie; Broken Hill

Jaroslav

Kalgoorlie; Broken Hill, NSW, January 1970–December 1975

How huge the moon had been over Kalgoorlie's lunar landscape, how wide and empty the land spewed out by its alien light. Broken Hill's moon too was expansive, illuminating the wide, empty land filled with mineral wealth and opportunity for those who knew how to take them, tearing and grinding from the rock. Not a welcoming land, glaring hard and cold in that fierce white light, or scorched dry beneath a fiercer sun. Yet there was a promise, a future, a life earned by muscle and sweat, not words. A place where a fair go stood for philosophy and idealism.

The Croatian Club there welcomed me with many questions where I had lived, what was my work, who I had known? I told them little of my life in Zagreb, nothing of Damir. I did not know to trust them. I read the papers, news three weeks a month old, news of the riots and the police and the army in my lost city. After some time I stopped reading the papers, stopped going to the club, started drinking at the pub with my Aussie workmates. They 'stirred' me, called me 'an ignorant wog' and 'a bloody Balt', but let me shout my round.

Such uncomplicated good humoured acceptance, such resolute indifference to anything outside the footy and the cricket, and the races and two-up was easier to swallow than the heavy richness of nostalgia, the endless political arguments at the club. Asked why he left, he simply said 'I am learning to be dinkum Aussie. I'm not Croatian now, I'm New Australian.'

Even as a 'wog' or 'bloody Balt', out there in the monotony of heat and dust, sweat and noise, digging and drilling and blasting he was not alone. By day, part of a drilling team; at night the moon's icy beacon lit the tumbled landscape, washed away the lumps and hollows, marking a precarious path. There in the monochrome shadows would be one or two men like him seeking a new life or a short reprieve, the risks and rewards there for those who knew how to take them.

The Graveyard

St Stephen's Cemetery, Church Street, Newtown, April 1978

The kids are in the graveyard behind St Stephen's church.
Colonial shipmasters, wrecked travellers, politicians,
businessmen, musicians and a poet or two
lie buried there. Early townsfolk, their wives,
and so many children. Babies by the dozen,
named or unnamed, infants of two or three,
some who survived to six or eight before
their time ran out. In the long grass
beneath crumbling headstones or caged
behind rusting iron fences lie grave slabs
cracked and fallen. Bees hum industriously
around the admiral's wife's last home,
sweet murmurings and scented flight
purposeful in the hot noon.

The kids are in the graveyard. Wagging school.
What child hasn't, especially on a sunny day?
School's boring, Mum's at work, no one to see and tell.
Behind the six-foot sandstone walls caging the graves
gangs of kids, some as young as six or eight, gather
on the long grass. They lean together over the tilted
slab, cans of lighter fluid in their hands. The damp
green's not at risk, they're not lighting grass
fires for a bit of juvenile fun.

The kids are in the graveyard sniffing petrol for the buzz.
The high comes as fumes float through dirty hankies or
lifted shirt-tails held over mouth and nose. The buzz can
be terrific. But it's never enough. Some kids use a can
a day. Six cans a week. And sometimes the buzz is bad.
Terrifying, hallucinatory, violent. The shopkeepers know,
when the kids buy lighter fluid day after day after day. They
don't want to see the sweating, the sores around the nose
and mouth, the terrors. They'd rather pretend the kids are
'just kids' out to light a few fires.

The kids are in the Children's Court. Pocket money
doesn't stretch to six cans a week. So petty larceny,
breaking and entering are added to the charge of
truancy. There's no charge for petrol sniffing, apart
from what physiology pays: brains, livers, lungs,
hearts, rotted; personalities and happiness gone.
They're not allowed to buy ciggies – too young for
that addiction, but they can buy, no questions
asked, fluid for the lighters that feed
the adults' hourly need for nicotine.

The cans are in the graveyard. They lie there in full sight
empty, beneath the gnarled Moreton Bay fig guarding
the gate to the churchyard: a dozen here, ten scattered
by the honey-scented tomb, more tossed under a rose
bush. The everyday violence of a stressed depressed
community litters the ground where already so many
children lie. An anguished mother pleads for help; her
tears unanswered. Police, the courts do nothing.
There's no law against sniffing petrol.

In Croatia

Jaroslav
Zagreb, Croatia, June 1967

Eight hundred years of glorious history surrounded us
but what we sought was our future. We climbed
the ramparts, ran laughing up the cobbled streets,
cathedral and castle, churches and cafes;
the town was our territory, the river banks
our playground. That shining summer
we spent our days on the cusp of life and love
and death hiding behind people's eyes
and in their words.

If we didn't think about politics, if we read
and studied and laughed and danced and sang,
if we dreamed of love and drank beer and wine
and the sweet plum liqueur and picnicked
with our friends in the park by the river
sharing good bread, sausages, cheese and fruit;
the girls brought peaches, plums, apricots,
cherries, music and sunshine, laughter and song,
flowers dancing, trees nodding in the breeze,
little white clouds dotting the blue.
The singing Sava ran through our town and
life as a student was good, if
you didn't think about politics.

If you didn't think about politics – but who
cannot think about politics when you are young
and idealistic and your country is at war? At war
with itself, communists and nationalists squabbling
who were the patriots? Who should run the country?
Who cannot think of politics when the squabbling
turns to gunfire and bomb blasts? When it's not safe
to voice your thoughts? Friends and lovers may be trusted,
but what of the others?

What of the people in the park by the river, beside
the flower beds, beneath the trees, under the white clouds
dotting that blue blue sky? Who was
listening? Who was watching? Who?
Husbands and wives, children, grandparents, lovers walking
hand in hand, people walking their dogs,
elderly women sitting alone with their knitting,
business men in grey suits, men in dark over-
coats, army officers? Who?

An International Village

Advertising feature in *The Newtown Voice Pictorial Weekly*, Saturday, 21 January 1978

An International Village

Welcome to the International Shopping
Village! What a pleasure it is to walk

along King Street, hearing as you pass the
music of many different countries. Your

nostrils tingle with aromas – moussaka
from a nearby Greek café, smoked salami

and exotic cheeses from the Continental
delis, the delightful smell of doner as it

turns on the spit of your local Turkish
lunch house. To follow, try a sticky Greek

pastry from the station café or a cake
from the nearby bakery, Continental or

Australian. Truly Newtown has become
a real International Shopping Village!

On the corner of King and Georgina, it's
The Salona Bar-Bistro-Restaurant. Open

seven days, seven nights from 11.30 a.m.
to 3 a.m. the next day. (Are they Greek?

Yugoslavs? Croatian? Who knows?) You
can cook your own steaks or souvlaki

(lamb skewers with capsicum and onions,
marinated in wine), or be daring and try

Continental-style sausages or fish.
All the salad you can eat! Dance

in the evenings to music (unspecified
but probably ethnic). The Salona is

handily placed close to Number 2
Fitzroy Street. (Upstairs, the Salona

may be a gambling den. Who knows?
Only the Greeks or Yugoslavs who

own it. Or maybe they're Croatians.)
Further down on King at number 168

is Nicholas Bros. Despite their Aussie
sounding name they import fine leather

shoes, both ladies' and men's, from
their Keffalonian home. Ladies' shoes

and unisex Indian sandals can also be
bought at Cono Markets a block along,

and there you can buy at bargain base-
ment prices Onkaparinga blankets (an

Aussie name to twist migrants' tongues).
Turning left on Wilson we leave 'the

Continent' (that's Europe) and head
into the Far East to a newly opened

restaurant, Yang Bin Fang. That's
Korean. How exotic! And authentic

Chinese cuisine can be enjoyed at
the Nanking Restaurant on the corn-

er of Missenden Road and King,
opposite the Marlborough Hotel.

On a celebratory note we read
the Greek Festival will be held

at the Centre, and an invitation
from the Yugoslav community

to 'people of all nationalities
to an Australia Day bash' at

Petersham Town Hall. There'll be
singing and dancing (Greek and
Yugoslav), and food and wine.

In Brief

A recent census lists the migrant
groups in Newtown's population:

Greeks, seven point five per cent,
Yugoslavs, five point six, Aussies

sixty-seven point six. (The rest,
it seems, invisible, not worth

counting. Perhaps their food
and music's not yet to our taste.)

Damir

Jaroslav

Jarun, Croatia, 20 April 1968

To evade those prying eyes, those hungry ears
Damir and I would ride the tram nine
kilometres south-west to the lake
where we could stretch out on the grass
and be private. The village of Jarun
was close, but not so close
we could be overlooked, overheard.
Damir would stand on a boulder declaiming
his poetry and I would lie on my back or sit,
arms around my knees listening, his words
against the calling of a distant bird, my cigarette
smoke curling to the sky.

Damir would not, could not keep
his thoughts to himself or whispered
to his friends. He stitched them into his poems
in steel sharp words like sewing needles,
phrases raking like machine-gun fire.
He was so beautiful: those wide bright eyes
and curling light brown hair, his footballer's legs
his wandering hands, his kisses. If I could
have stopped him writing, speaking, stopped
him with my mouth, my hands, my body.
But my love was not enough,
could not compete with his country.
That day with our friends in the basement

bookshop where we read the latest books,
Damir reciting, softly, from the manuscript
of his new poems. About sunset we left,
walking upstairs to the street, arm in arm
he and I. But the doorway is narrow,
I let him go ahead. A crack
of rifle fire and he is sprawled
across the cobblestones.
No time to grieve. A flash of light, a crash,
the shop is bombed and burning.
Marco and I running down
narrow back streets scorched,
terrified,
alive.

Scoop!

Tom

King Street, Newtown, the night of Thursday, 16 February 1978

I come around the corner to the taste
of smoke, of burning rubber and petrol
on the night air. Falling cinders smudge
my face, my eyes burn with the haze.
I've been disco dancing down at the Hub,
and I'm walkin home to clear my head
of music and booze and ciggie smoke, of girls
in flashy dresses and too much makeup
and the Greeks and Turks in their too tight jeans
leerin at the girls and leerin at me. Christ!
This is huge! The Rural Bank an the jeweller's,
an several other buildings, like somethin from
photos of the Blitz! Fire bombed and still alight.

Broken glass under my shoes and the boots
of the cops and fireys inching toward
the burning bank. Black smoke in the night
air. Some of the firies've got breathing equipment
– wish I did, though I'm just a gawping bystander.
There's a gaping hole in the bank's roof,
timber trusses smoking. Funny, the pale stars
sparking through the gap calm and serene.

Geez, look at these two cars! Gotta take notes, this one's a front-page screamer for sure – the fuck's my camera? The Ed'll have a fit I was here and couldn't get shots to splash across the front. (No good telling him I was discoing – no excuse.
If he'd his way, I'd have my camera everywhere
I went – even to bed. Especially to bed!)

Jeez those cars've really copped a blast. They
sit on bare rims, tyres puddled, the glass
from windscreens and windows diamonds
spilled across the road an footpath. Their
paintwork's psychedelic metal greens and blues
burned back to patterns of brownish black.
And a third car, on its side, skewed
across the road and gutter. I move closer,
jotting notes. The whole front of the bank torn
away. Counters and filing cabinets twisted
and blackened, drawers scattered across
the floor, their contents piles of smoking ash.
The joint's still smouldering though the fireys
have doused the flames. Smoke trails down
what's left of the staircase from a jagged hole
in the ceiling. I peer up and see charred wood,
the manager's scorched desk, his leather-look
vinyl chair a melted shapeless blob an twisted
steel stark against the black night sky.

Loud comments from across the road:
I swing around. A bunch of people
sticky-beakin like me, from a safer
distance. Three women in nothing much
at all carryin on about the twisted iron fence
and upstairs windows smashed by the blast.
The men with them hail a passing cab
and get away quick smart.

Another cab comes by, slowing to gawk,
I whistle an hop in, get him to wait
while I dash into my flat, grab my
camera and flash and rush me
back to take some pics before the cops
tell me to hop it. The Ed will be pleased.
Shots and time to develop them
before we go to press.

My scoop! Front page! Three
of my photos blown up real big.
It's true it's been a slowish week
and we're a weekly rag, but mine's
a hummer of a yarn, my bomb blast
coming just three days after the Hilton
in George street copped a bomb,
with all those foreign nobs. They say
that's down to the Ananda Marga.
Maybe mine is too. I can see the headline:
Mad bombers in Australia!

Break-in black-out

Front page of *The Newtown Voice*, Wednesday 23 March 1978

BREAK-IN BLACKOUT –
SHOPKEEPERS AFRAID

A shopkeeper whose premises were broken into twice last week fears any publicity over the break-ins.

'Publish something in the paper,' he said, 'and they'll be back to break in again.' The black-out on news

of the event extends even to the Newtown Police, in whose area the shop is sited. Inspector Rob Daly,

the Officer in Charge of Newtown, said there had been no report to police of the break-ins. It is reliably

reported that the glass shopfront was smashed on two consecutive nights last week. A nearby shopkeeper

commented that the shop 'had more than its fair share of trouble lately'. This is just one instance that has

come to the attention of *The Voice* recently of the high level of FEAR that pervades Newtown. On the surface

everything is fine, but go under the surface and even the most respected Newtown shopkeepers are afraid.

Afraid of being bombed, as happened to Sterns Jewellers and the Rural Bank, or being burned out

as has happened to other shops which have mysteriously caught fire. The King Street Bomber

is still at large, the Dulwich Hill Fire Bug still roams the streets. 'Who is next?' they ask.

How I met Harry

Buzz

At the Town Hall Hotel, King Street, Newtown, Thursday evening,
18 December 1977

The WEA put on a Chrissie party this evenin
after class, so us casual teachers can meet
each other an have a bit of Xmas cheer. It
was in the big seminar room; someone'd

hung Chrissie decorations from the neon light
covers, an there was an Xmassy paper cloth
on the table, an red an green paper serviettes
for the cabanossi chunks and bitsa cheese an

pineapple stuck together on toothpicks an the
sausage rolls an Xmas mince pies. Some
smartarse had spiked the punch with sweet
sherry – a whole flagon from the taste of it –

pretty bloody awful. I didn't know anyone much,
so was just drinkin a bit an checkin everyone out
when in comes this tall girl, long red hair tied in
a ponytail, legs that look like they go all the way

up. I'd seen her a coupla times, passing me in the
corridor. Time to stop pervin an go chat to her. Hi,
I'm Buzz an I teach car maintenance, what d'ya
teach? Turns out her name's Harry an she's only

been teachin paintin for a few weeks. Doesn't
know anyone in Sydney. Where d'ya live, I ask.
Launceston, I mean I used to, I live in Newtown
now. Newie! How about that! I live there too!

How about we dump outta this borin Xmas crap
an go an find a real drink? So we ended up
in the Townie cos it's the nearest pub to the
station. We hadn't had much to eat apart from

the handful of cabanossi whatsits I grabbed on
the way out, so with a coupla cups of that
godawful punch we were both pretty giggly on
the train back to Newie. The beers at the pub

helped us 'push the boat out further'. That's her
expression. Posh, isn't it? By ten o'clock I was
feelin' really frisky an although I was tryin to
focus on what she was tellin me about her

paintin, I just wanted to eat her. So I leaned
in an gave her a big wet smackeroo. She pulled
away, but slowly, like she was bein tactful, an
moved a bit further along the seat. God, I'm

sorry; stupid of me; I was red an hot, so stupid.
Sorry, sorry! Can I get ya another beer? No, she
says, I think I'd better go. Can I walk ya home?
(I wanted to see where she lived.) No thanks, it's

only a few blocks. So here I am, nursing me beer,
feelin sorry for myself. Then I brighten up. It's only
a few weeks till WEA starts again, an then I'll see
her twice a week. An maybe run into her on King Street.

Mugging Patrols

From *The Newtown Voice*, Wednesday, 30 March 1978

Mugging Patrols

Sixteen violent crimes – mostly beatings and muggings – have been reported to police over the past two weeks.

The crimes were mainly committed in or near hotels around closing time, Insp. Rob Daly, Officer in Charge of Newtown

Police, told *The Voice*. He warned that the numbers of attacks occurring outside pubs at closing time is at an alarming level,

with 'blood in the streets', particularly in Enmore Road. Most of the attacks in Enmore Rd were in the vicinity of

the Duke, the Sly Fox, and the Warren View hotels. The Warren View is particularly dangerous, Insp. Daly said.

Violent attacks frequently take place in the hotel toilets and on the street. He warned people to take extra care

when entering or leaving any of these establishments, or walking past them after dark. Police have stepped up

their patrols along Enmore Road, King Street and Erskineville Road. The spate of physical attacks is causing fear and people are

taking steps to defend themselves. The recently opened Rape Crisis Centre in Chippendale has started weekly self

defence classes, partly funded by South Sydney Council. In addition, Cr Joe Meissner has taken out half-page adverts

proclaiming his prowess as 'never-defeated World Open Karate Champion'. Cr Meissner offers a crash course in

unarmed combat, 'no need to be fit or experienced'.

An undercurrent of corruption

Front-page Comment in *The Newtown Voice*, Wednesday, 7 June 1978

AN UNDERCURRENT OF CORRUPTION

An undercurrent of corruption runs through Newtown, and occasionally it surfaces.

Allegations have been made about stand-over tactics, bashings, hard drugs, gambling, bomb threats even. But

nobody has come forward with hard evidence. There are believed to be two statutory declarations in existence,

from people claiming to have been threatened and abused. *The Voice* has not seen either declaration. When approached

to vouch for the story, several people said they 'wouldn't touch it with a 40-foot pole'. Allegations have been made

that people are afraid of intimidation. We've been told if we pursue the story that we'll likely get a bomb through the window. It's hard to penetrate Newtown's wall of silence.

The Greeks North & South (1)

Tom

North and South King Street, Newtown, Saturday, 20 May 1978

A week after we'd dined at Ellenika
I thought I'd take Harry slummin
down South King Street to see some more
of the migrant life of Newtown. Not that
she's a migrant really, it's only a hop
from the Apple Isle to the big smoke.
But there's things you wouldn't see in
Tassie; it never hurts to impress a girl
with knowledge of what goes on,
the seamier side of big city life.

I met Harry (Harriet really, but for some
chick reason she prefers Harry) at the disco
coupla weeks ago. She was with a blonde
girl – name of Buzz – (another stupid chick
name). I spotted right away Buzz was
a lezzo. So when this red-headed girl said
I'm Harry, I thought gawd, another one!
But when I got her on the dance floor
she was wigglin her hips an making eyes
at me, something more than the music
was turnin her on.

She's a good lookin chick, and when we
went for dinner to a Greek restaurant
a few nights later I saw she'd dressed up
for me. A nice green dress showed off
her curves and matched her eyes (I
saw they were green straight off), high
heels, perfume, dinky chick's bag. I'd
scrubbed up too, my best suit – the grey
one with red and blue sparks like tiny
neon lights in the weave – white shirt, red
paisley tie, sapphire cufflinks (not real
on my pay, but flash enough to impress
a bird on the first date). My car's hot too –
electric blue Falcon, only five years old,
goes like a cut cat, always turns heads
at the lights. My old man woulda said
I was flash as a rat with a gold tooth.

We had the works when I took Harry to Ellenika,
the whole damn slap-up authentic Greek cuisine.
The dips with flat bread, pickled octopus, souvlaki,
nice wine, white tablecloths, silver cutlery, candles.
Blue an white walls, posters of the Parthenon,
fishin boats, windmills, bouzouki music playin
on a tape. All that full-on Greek shit. Gets
them every time. I think she was impressed.

I told her about my job as deputy editor
of *The Newtown Voice*. There's always somethin
to write up, somethin to chase. The other week
my car chase led page three. I'd been workin late,
layin up the ads, when I caught the call on
the scanner, a bunch of teenagers joy-ridin
in a stolen Holden. I shot out to the Falcon, raced
down City Road, caught them on Parramatta,
just before the turn-off to Petersham. The cop
car screamed up, siren howlin, blue light
strobin, the little buggers panicked, swung
left, crashed into the shop window on the corner.

It was a ripper chase, I had my camera, got good
shots of the crash, the cops pullin the stupid gits
out of the car and cuffin em. Made a good page
three lead. We go for drama, pics beef up a yarn
– but I was pipped for the cover by an old lady
run over in the supermarket car park. *The Voice*'s
always gonna run with crime and teenage hoons,
old women getting knocked over and fears about
community safety. That and the worries about
the wogs. A good reporter loves his job (apart
from crap stuff like layin up the bloody ads).

I don't just cover the day to day stuff – the
fires, break-ins, hoons nickin cars, council
meetings – though I do all that; there's
just me and the Ed puttin *The Voice*
to bed each week. I'm an investigative
journalist, and there's lots to investigate
in dirty old Newie – gamblin and prossies
an the Medibank fraud, gang warfare
an drugs – and somehow the migrants
have got a finger in every bit of it.

In Newtown

Jaroslav

Hordern Street, Newtown, May 1977

Weary, so weary I sit, the train rattles over the points, hands between my knees, eyes closed. 10.30, shift done, all I want is to go home. Home. Where is that? Not Newtown, Kalgoorlie, Broken Hill. The singing Sava, the vine-covered hills around my city, the cathedral, the parks, bookshops and little bars, the streets and laneways – all gone, long gone. My youth, my friends, all gone. Damir dead. Dead and buried in my heart. This place where I keep my clothes, books, bed, and drink my coffee, is just a place, a space to fill the time between daylight work and the longing night. I don't read my books now. Sometimes I take one, lovingly, hold it to my face, sniffing for some trace of Damir and my life before this.

Stumbles to the kitchen, measures coffee, sugar, water into a briki, lights the stove, sits copper pan on the flame, takes off the frothing liquid, stirs it, puts back on, takes it off, stirs, on again, three times, pours carefully into his tiny porcelain cup. On the back step, empty cup beside him, facing down the yard to sagging clotheslines, rolls a cigarette, hands working automatically, eyes on the sliver of moon tacked to the cardboard sky backdrop to the brick dunny.

I should have gone to the club instead of coming here. Bright lights, music, people drinking, laughing, shouting, the company of fellow Croats. No! Not there! I should have stayed in the city, gone to the bar, gone to Hyde Park, found myself someone for the night.

I was a fool to come back to this.

The moon that lit his path so brightly in Broken Hill shines furtively, shamefaced here. Above the harbour it swings high and free, at ease over rich men's houses, gardens, yachts, but the inner west's dirty streets and cramped backyards have shrunk it, made unsure of its welcome. Even in Hyde Park, with the fountain's tinkle and the sweet narcotic scent from flower beds and cigarettes, inky shadows bloom that the moon seems to shun.

How can I ever be at home here on the far side of the world, here on the dark side of the moon?

Lock the toilets

From *The Newtown Voice*, Wednesday, 7 June 1978

Lock the Toilets

Public toilets should be closed at night to avoid any public nuisance, according to Petersham councillor Ken Broad,

speaking at last week's Marrickville Council meeting. Problems were caused by the homosexuals, he said, who

frequented toilet blocks after dark. 'I don't have anything against homosexuals,' Cr Broad told *The Voice*, 'but

problems develop from their activities.' Asked what were the problems he declined to answer, but stressed 'we've got

to stop these people loitering in the toilets in the late hours of the night. Homosexuals regularly gathered in groups at

Petersham Park,' he said, 'and could appear threatening to other people wishing to use the park or its toilets. Toilet

blocks in Marrickville, Erskineville, Enmore and Newtown are well known as magnets for homosexuals,' he added.

If Cr Broad's suggestion is taken up, all the district's public toilets will be locked after dark.

The Yowie

Buzz

At Harry's, King Street, Newtown, Wednesday, 19 July 1978

Gough promised us free education but
Gough's not in charge any more, so
it won't be free for long. Not much is,
(cept love, an that's not free for all,

Only for straights like you). Anyhow
what's the use of free education if
you've got nowhere to live? Sydney
Uni's a giant Yowie hiding in its sand-

Stone castle. When we're not looking
it crawls into our neighbourhood, into
our Darlington, chews up our streets,
crunchin up homes with its iron jaws,

Swallowin the lives, lines, laneways,
memories of us workin-class people.
My mum knows people, people she
grew up with, went to school with,

People who lived all their lives two,
three streets away. Their houses
knocked down, streets dug up
to make room for classrooms and

Lecture halls. Livin squashed in
with luckier rellies, kids shared
among nannas, aunts, cousins.
Some campin in the Rest Park or

Like me, squattin wherever the uni
an the council don't see us. There's
lots of empty buildins around. Fact-
ories, warehouses; some even belong

To the uni, some the council control.
Why can't the Yowie munch on its own
buildins if it's so hungry? Why can't
the council sell its empty buildins for

The uni to knock down an build their
classrooms? Why pick on us, make us
homeless? The bastards! It's class warfare,
that's what it is. Fuckin class warfare! Well,

We're fightin' back. Squattin's the go.
Good thing about some of these empty
places the council and the uni forget,
they're easy to break into an big enough

To make a home for six or ten or more
of us. 'Course you have to be fit an fast
on your feet an good with your hands
to live in an Anarchist squat, an not be

Afraid of the dark. You'd be too soft, Harry.
But thanks for the hot shower an the nice
meal an the very drinkable plonk. We should do
this again some night. Waddya reckon, kiddo?

Staring at the Upward

Harry

Art Gallery of NSW, Sydney, Sunday, 2 November 1977

I spent a long time staring at
the painting, trying to absorb
the artist's technique – his thick
broad swoop, one brushstroke
of dark blackish-green curving
from mid-baseline to two-thirds
up, exploding in arms of blood
or fire stretched like Christ's on

a non-existent cross, drops spat-
tering the ground black-green-
red. Surry Hills Green. 1960.
Peter Upward. Non-figurative.
Maybe it was aerial: petrol spill-
ing onto tarmac turning blood
into flames. It's the urgency,
the force of the artist's vision

driving through his hand to
his brush to canvas to me.
I sketch and resketch with oil
pastels, I jot notes, arrows,
I make colour blocks. Trying
to capture the techniques, tics
and tricks that bring oil paint
on canvas to singing life. Stiff,

eyes sore, I put my sketchbook
down, go out for fresh air and
a smoke. On a bench in the sun
sat the handsome European
man. Hello, I said, mind if I sit
here? We met the other week.
We chatted about the painting.
Ah yes, the very hot dry town.

Drysdale, you said. I thought it
amusing that a man with such
a name should paint such a place.
I hadn't thought of that, I said,
that's funny. My name's Harriet,
most people call me Harry. He
took my hand and bowed over it.

My pleasure, Harry. I am Jaroslav,
but you may call me Jaro.
Most people do not. We sat
smoking, no talking. When I
got up, he said, perhaps we could
walk across the park, the Domain,
and sit in the sun? There's a kiosk
where one may buy a coffee.

We sat on metal chairs
and Jaro asked about my paint-
ing, so I told him about leaving
Rod and coming to Sydney and
having to teach at WEA to make
ends meet, and how hard it was.
And you, I asked, remembering

my manners, why did you leave
your home to come to Sydney?
He was silent for so long I was
afraid I'd offended him, then he
sighed. There was civil war. Much
shooting and bombing. My best
friend was killed. I must leave

or be arrested, imprisoned,
shot, who knows? So I come
to Australia to get away, to be
Australian, not Croat, to make
a new life. He sighed again.
I didn't know what to say.

We're both making new lives,
you and me, Jaro, new homes,
new lives. He sighed again,
bowed slightly and shook my
hand. I left him there and went
back to stare at the Upward.

Bets Raid

Front page of *The Newtown Voice*, Wednesday 9 August 1978

BETS RAID
36 people arrested

Despite a DIV 21 raid, *The Voice* notes an illegal gambling club in Enmore is still operating. On the 1st floor of 159

Enmore Road, the 'Enmore Greek Social Club' has three poker machines, and offers patrons free beer and coffee.

Temporary council consent to operate as a coffee lounge ran out two weeks ago. The fight with Marrickville Council to

operate as a coffee lounge has been going on for several months. Council has been reluctant to give consent, citing

inadequate off-street parking. Also, more importantly, because 74 per cent of the total floor area was not going

to be used for coffee. The club's lawyer told Council 'there was lively competition among the Greek business community,

leading to gossip' by one rival against another. Council gave the club six months permission to operate; this ran out on

July 26. Fourteen days later, the 'Enmore Greek Social Club' is still in operation.

The Greeks North & South (2)

Tom

South King Street, Newtown, Saturday, 20 May 1978

Yep, we had the works when we went to Ellenika.
This time it's gonna be different. So we drive
down the bottom end of King Street almost to
Speeders, to this little Greek café in a ratty
two-storey building, yiros an chiko rolls
and milkshakes downstairs, an upstairs?
That's what we were gonna check out. I
told her last week that it's my job to know
what's goin on under the table, and to let
the wogs know that I know, that I'm
watchin them. They all want to keep on
my good side, the paper's good side.
They don't want us pokin around – which
is what I do as a reporter – they want us
just to write up their delis, butchers,
restaurants, shoe shops, tailoring,
coffee roasters, whatever, so that
us real Aussies will buy their goods,
eat in their restaurants, drink their
coffee, and not look too closely at how
they do their business an make a quid,
an what goes on upstairs an after dark.

The set-up's your usual wog milkbar-café, laminex counter, yiros grills, plastic bowls of sliced tomatoes, shredded lettuce, sliced onions, pink, green an blue milkshake containers, glass oven with pies an pasties, chiko rolls, espresso machine topped with tiny cups, cake case with baklava and other pastries. You get the picture. We had yiros, what the Turks call doner kebabs, an I ordered coffee an some pastries. I know chicks like somethin sweet, an a coffee an cake should sweeten Harry so she'll agree to go upstairs with me. I want to see if what I guess is right.

Gambling Terror

Front page of *The Newtown Voice*, Wednesday, 16 August 1978

GAMBLING TERROR
MOBSTER REIGN OF VIOLENCE

Gambling mobsters have cowed Marrickville aldermen
and business people into silence. It is well-known that

particular premises are operating as gambling joints,
and that some are run by big-time competing mobsters.

Occasionally the rivalry breaks out into open warfare. This
is believed to be behind the recent bombing of premises

in Newtown some months ago. In addition, shock waves
are still reverberating after a particularly gruesome murder

early last week. Initially firemen thought there was nobody
in the house totally destroyed by fire. Then they found a

man's body stuffed under a bed. The throat had been cut,
and the person had been shot and stabbed several times.

It is believed to have been an underworld deal involving
rival gambling interests. The event has terrorised small

operators around the district. We spoke to several people
last week, but no one dared to be quoted. They said they

would not take the risk. They said they had wives and
children to look after, and were frightened of what would

happen. They said they were 'getting knocked off' in police
raids, but that 'the big boys' were getting away scot-free.

The reaction to our queries every time was 'I don't know any
thing. Leave me out of this.' It was perfectly clear they did

know more than they were saying – but were afraid to
talk. Marrickville councillors are also running scared.

One commented, 'Do you want to get me circumcised?'
Another said there were 'some heavyweights around.

I've heard some funny stories.' But he wasn't telling any.
Another said one place had been closed down after brawls

in which people had been thrown out first-storey windows
and blood ran in the gutters. He said he knew of one case

where gambling interests had 'stood over' an alderman, who
was 'quite worried' about it. (He is no longer an alderman.)

Several councillors commented on the 'hypocrisy' and
'inconsistency' in the way in which gambling premises

were treated, but refused to elaborate further.
Once again, the wall of silence descends.

At the WEA

Harry

Workers' Education Association (WEA) building, Kent Street,
Sydney, Thursday, 6 November 1977

I can't believe I conned them
the staff at WEA, that I could teach as well
as paint. So let's see how this works. Two
nights a week I teach people how to do what
I struggle to achieve the rest of my week –
create something good from my daily grind.
People who might have some talent (whatever
that means), or not. Either they've got some-
thing inside and it'll come out, or they haven't.

I can't bloody put into them
what they haven't already got. I know I'm not
a teacher's elbow, although I have to kid them
I am if I want to get paid. So I walk around look-
ing at people's work trying to be encouraging,
offering a helpful suggestion now and then, but
god, if they really can't paint why do they come
to a painting class? It's not something you can
really teach, you just have to do it day after day

after day and go on doing it,
just keep working at it until it comes right or
you give up on it, start something new. Or
go away. Try something else, something differ-
ent like crocheting or car maintenance. That
girl there, what's her name, Rosemary, she's
got a good feel for colour but her brushwork's
pathetic. But she keeps on coming and looks
like she's been trying it at home.

Persistence. She'll dig it out of herself
with those gouging strokes. Here, let me
show you a trick with the palette knife.
Lay the paint on thick like you're plastering a wall,
see? Then take the knife's edge and cut it through.
Make a line – make your line – here take the knife.
That's it. Also, see, you can use the edge
to scrape some colour off, clean it right back or
just enough to get the depth you need.

Right-oh, class, nine o'clock. That's it
for another week. Don't forget to take all your
things. Tomorrow night's class is conversational
Japanese and they're so very tidy-minded. The
theme for next week? Right. OK, let's see…
something from your past. Am I glad to see them go!
Now I'd love a drink. It's pretty bloody depressing
being single and broke with no one to drink with. Oh,
hello, Jaro!
What a pleasant surprise!

Vice squad acts

Front page of *The Newtown Voice*, Wednesday, 7 June 1978

VICE SQUAD ACTS
Investigation into Massage Parlour

The vice squad has closed down the massage parlour
in Fitzroy Street, but already two new ones have opened,

one in Mallet Street, the other in Marian Street. The vice
squad raided the parlour on the same day *The Voice*

published our front-page exposé. After the raid, a woman
was charged with soliciting in a massage parlour. The raid

followed complaints from local businesses about the parlour
in Fitzroy Street. The Chamber of Commerce had written to

South Sydney Council and Newtown Police, citing heavy congestion in the narrow street. Some local businessmen want

the parlour closed. They have appealed several times to
Council to get rid of it, but Council say they can do nothing

about it. The proprietor of a nearby concern said that
'professional men are moving into the area and historic

buildings are being restored. The massage parlour' (in a
Victorian terrace house) 'is detracting from the area's

reputation.' Later, he called *The Voice* asking us not
to use his name saying, 'It's just not worth the hassle.'

Sauna mystery

From *The Newtown Voice*, Wednesday, 21 June 1978
(No byline, but probably written by Tom)

Sauna Mystery

It seemed to amuse the Newtown locals to see a sauna bath, complete with dials and electric plug, reposing sedately in

Fitzroy Street, last Thursday evening, leaning against a No Standing sign. Nothing unusual, you say; this is Newtown.

But the No Standing sign is only yards from the front door of the famous No 2 Fitzroy Street, well publicised recently

for 'home comforts' allegedly available there. These home comforts were consistently advertised in *The Voice*, but with

pressure from the Newtown Chamber of Commerce the premises were shut down two weeks ago, their operations

transferred to premises in Mallett Street. No 2 was then renovated and painted out very nicely, apparently returned

to 'normal use' as a residence for people. But not much has changed: stories reaching *The Voice* indicate that the girls

have been plying their trade from cars in that street, and that Fitzroy Street is back in operation again. Even so,

it's bold, even for Newtown, to lay on saunas in the street. Unfortunately, when your intrepid reporter went back to get

a picture, the sauna had been moved – back inside perhaps? You never know, maybe the Council Clean-up arrived in time

to give our Eskimo Nell garbos some 'home comforts'.

Tin Shed Girls

Buzz

Harry's place, King Street, Newtown, Friday, 28 April 1978

There's some bolshie girls at the Tin
Sheds, Harry, the kind I like. A
few OK fellas too, but the girls are
really somethin. They're challengin

The system with their WAM – that's
Women's Art Movement – you'd like
that, Harry. They're not doin arty
farty stuffy elitist art, they're re-

Claimin traditional women's stuff
– crochet an embroidery, doilies –
sounds poncy but it isn't cos it's
political, stuff about women's place

In the social fabric, how women's
work is undervalued, devalued. How
the personal is political. Good stuff,
eh? There's some really bolshie girls

In that lot. I was walking behind one
yesterday. She wore tight jeans I could-
n't take my eyes off. Sweet round
cheeks like warm peaches. I followed

Her three blocks before she turned
down a side street… Anyhow, as
well as bein hot chicks an anarchists
an feminists, these girls – an the guys

They hang out with – all artists – run fab-
ulous gigs; well, they do ripper posters
for discos an fundraisers for battered
women an shelters an antiwar demos

In Darlington an Chippo an Newie an some
times down at the Tin Sheds. I reckon you an
me oughta go to one. Have some fun an meet
some of these artist types. Waddya reckon?

The Dream

Jaroslav

Hordern Street, Newtown, May 1978

I'm in my bed. I know I am asleep. I know I'm dreaming. But my flesh and bones drag me where I know I cannot be. Beside the singing river. Laughing and dancing with Marco and Milo, Damir and the girls, Anneke and Elsibet, drinking wine and beer. I raise my glass. A crow flies up to a branch of the elm. Damir and I are in the hills behind Jarun. He climbs a crag, declaims a poem, falls. His head splits open, brains and blood puddle down the rock. The white hard rock my pickaxe bites into. My hands are calloused and sweaty. My neck is burned by the sun. The men with me joke and swear in their rough Aussie way. The moon pours a path bone white between those darkened boulders. A man waits for me in the cleft. He gestures across the grass under the green domed trees. He's walking towards the toilet block. I reach to take his hand. I'm on my hands and knees before Damir, the ground heaves. Burning books cascade over me.

The Subterranean Bar

Harry

Kent Street, Sydney, Thursday, 27 November 1977

When Jaro picked me up at WEA that night
he took me to a bar a few blocks away, down
a steep flight of steps beneath a jeweller's
shop. He put his hand under my elbow as
we walked, and going down the stairs he put
his hand on my arm to steady me. It felt
strange, and good, to have a strong masculine
presence – a strong masculine scent – so close

after so long. The bar was tiny, three tables
two chairs apiece. Jaro nodded to the owner,
who brought a bottle of white wine from under
the counter. I thought we'd be drinking red,
like everyone does. Croatian wine, Jaro said,
very good. It was light but kind of aromatic,
like it had herbs in it. Cheers, I said. *Živeli!*
he replied. Your very good health. After that,

we met quite often. He would wait for me out-
side the WEA, and we'd walk, his hand under
my elbow, along the street and down the stairs,
always his arm guiding me carefully, into the little
subterranean bar. Our bar. We'd drink Croatian wine
and black coffee and smoke, and Jaro would tell me
about his life after he fled his country and came
to Australia. He made it sound exciting and amusing,

although I saw the sadness in his eyes.
He seemed determined to become an Aussie,
to leave his old life behind
on the other side of the world. One night, I said,
why don't we have dinner together?
I'll cook and you can look at my paintings.

Upstairs at Number 543

Harry

South King Street, Newtown, Saturday, 20 May 1978

After the yiros (not as good as last
week's souvlaki), Tom ordered
coffees and baklava and asked if we
could go upstairs. The owner smiled
but didn't seem too pleased. Is only
old people up there, play cards.
Not interesting for young couple
like you. Sit down and I put on
the Greek music. Maybe you like

dance? No, Tom said, we don't want
to dance. I put on my most charming
smile – the one I'd practised on the old
bats of Lonnie's A-list. I'm sorry, I fluted
in prissy lady tones, I'd love to stay
and listen to your music, but my friend
is so interested in people's customs,
what they do to relax, so… Okay, you go
up. Sit near back; I bring your coffee.

He followed us upstairs and guided us
to a table by a window at the back. A
dozen or so people playing cards, men
at one group of tables, women at another.
Collecting dirty cups and glasses, chatting
to the men, he bustled back down. Huh,
Tom muttered, they've been warned. We
won't see anything interesting now.

I took a bite of baklava; its sweetness
caught my throat and made me cough.

When I could breathe again, I saw the
women staring at me silently, making
no effort to hide their stares. Maybe
not used to having Australians in their
space? A moment or two; the chatter
rose again, those not playing, clicking
at their knitting. They talked loudly. I
couldn't catch a word. The players
shouted, laughed, groaned – winners

and losers clear in any tongue. Tom
leaned over, whispering as he passed
the cakes: look over there, don't move
your head, look, there's money changing
hands. I saw a man slip a folded note
to another as he was dealt a hand. A fiver,
Tom murmured. One man then threw down
his cards. He stood up, knocking a cup,
sepia liquid spilling. An older man
sitting next to him stood up, too, put

his hand on his arm, said something to
calm him. But the young man grew angrier,
swearing, and leaning forward, softly
threatened the dealer, then tipped
the table over. Everyone was shouting
and swearing; the women put down cards
and knitting to watch. Two players righted
the table, straightened the chairs, picked
up cards and coins off the floor. Women
resumed knitting. The storm seemed over.

The angry man turned, pulled out a knife
slashed at the dealer's arm, ripped the
sleeve, drew blood. A woman screamed.
More shouting, swearing. The hurt man
sat down, pale, his friend pulled out
a hankie, tied it to staunch the blood, the
angry one's friend urging him to put his
knife away. Together they walked towards
the stairs, the angry one turned back, made
a threatening gesture. The wounded man,

snarling, returned the gesture. Come on,
said Tom, time for us to get out. I was
glad to go. My legs were shaky, I nearly
fell down those narrow stairs. Out
on the street: Well, he said, you've had
a little taste of what goes on every day
in dirty, crooked Newtown. It's not
just foreign food and ethnic music.

Gambling clean-up

Front-page Comment *The Newtown Voice*, Wednesday, 23 August 1978

Gambling clean-up
Root out the crims!

The Voice's stories about gambling in the district have caused some rumblings of discontent among the gambling fraternity.

We have even heard of threats being issued. There are some big operators involved around Newtown-Marrickville. They

don't like their activities being brought to light. If the dogs are barking right, these people won't stop at bombings and

even murder. Let's face the issue squarely. Everyone knows there is widespread illegal gambling in the area. It isn't hard

to find. There are plenty of coffee lounges and social clubs with unauthorised poker machines on the premises. At least

there were, until *The Voice* got into the act. Now it's all strictly under the counter. You don't have to look too far

either if you want a flutter on the horses or the dogs outside the TAB. The police and aldermen know exactly where these

places are. One of them is right opposite a police station. Of course, coffee lounges and social clubs aren't the only places.

Everyone knows the SP boys are operating in some of the pubs. In fact, those who squeal the loudest about corruption

are among those most deeply involved in it. Like the Aussie publican who dobbed in a Greek gambling joint to us. Like the businessman who wants to 'clean up Newtown'. We know of at least two brothels he's supposed to own. We can't

comment on a heroin dealing charge to be heard shortly. But drugs seem to be part of the scene generally. Allegations of

drug trafficking were thrown around in a brothel story we did a few weeks ago. We are also aware of allegations about

drugs involving a businessman who is also active on the gambling scene. Let's get one thing clear. *The Voice* isn't

opposed to gambling as such, or even brothels. As far as we're concerned, it would be a hell of a lot better if both

activities were legalised and properly regulated. In fact, that's the only way to get rid of the corruption that currently

pervades the scene. Why should these activities be illegal in themselves? For some people it's a way of life, no more and

no less. For many Greeks and Yugoslavs, for example, gambling is as natural as two-up or beer to an Aussie.

Because of the insane nature of Australian gambling laws, decent people are being turned into criminals. We should legalise gambling and prostitution and root out the crims.

Yellowcake

Tom

Over a beer at the Courthouse Hotel, aka Courties, Australia Street, Newtown, Friday, 14 July 1978

Another ripper front page (though
the Ed cast his beady eye across it
to make sure I hadn't stuffed it up
before he wrote his Comment). It was
real cloak an dagger stuff: convoys of
radioactive uranium yellowcake racing
along narrow Newtown an Marrickville
streets before dawn, with no one know-
ing a thing about it. Seems neither the
Newtown cops nor Marrickville Council'd
been warned beforehand.

Council are keeping Mum; officially they
say they know nothin about the convoys.
Over the past week there's been at least
seven of em, fifteen trucks at a time,
carryin two hundred tonnes of radioactive
stuff, beltin along the Princes Highway
into Victoria Road, Enmore Road, Stanmore Road
an Liberty Street, an late one night a uranium
convoy was seen in Edgeware Road. Sheer
bloody luck there hasn't been an accident!

I could just see a bunch a hoons in a hot
wired car runnin a red light an crashin
into one of those convoys – huge pileup –
radioactive dust flyin every-bloody-where.
Contamination of a nation – at least Newie
an Marrickville, coulda bin a real disaster!
Council workers've had no trainin to deal
with dangerous substances like yellow-
cake, or even any protective gear. Bob
White (he's Shire Engineer) says any
mess would land on the plate of State
Emergency Service. They've got an office
in Newtown, but it's hardly ever open.

Front-page Comment *The Newtown Voice*, Wednesday, 12 July 1978

WHY THE SILENCE?

It reads like a James Bond thriller. Uranium convoys
roaring through the back streets of Newtown in the dead

of night, using a series of different routes. It's all being
done in secret, and nobody, but nobody, has been told

a thing about it. Except this isn't fiction, and if things go
wrong, it is we who will pay the price. The Federal

Government and the AAEC want to flog off our uranium,
and intend to do it regardless of public opinion. When

stories like this come to light, it looks like they intend to
do it regardless of public life. So concerned are they

to avoid publicity and the resultant demonstrations, that they're
even keeping in the dark people who should know,

if our homes are to be protected. The fact is that no provision has been made in the event of an accident. No doubt

the authorities will tell us that the risks are minimal. But
with 250 such smashes in the US since 1971, that seems

a pretty poor sort of argument. And we already have our
very own radioactive waste disposal problem at Hunters

Hill – and that stuff has lain there for more than half a
century. Now the residents have to move because of it.

Nobody is willing to admit responsibility for the uranium
convoys racing through Marrickville streets late at night;

Nobody knows what will happen if there is an accident.
All three levels of government simply refer enquiries

back to each other. It's like an endless piece of string.
What happens when that string breaks? Nobody knows.

Spag bol and cheesecake

Harry

King Street, Newtown, Thursday, 16 February 1978

When Jaro left, around eleven-thirty,
I couldn't settle down. It had been
so good, showing him my work, talking
too much about what I was trying to do
with my latest frustrating painting; telling
him about the students at WEA, making
him laugh about pushing Rod into the river.

It was good too, so good, having him sitting
at my table, eating my food, food I'd cooked
specially for him – though I made far too much
and I'll be eating it for days – and the frozen
cheesecake was OK, though probably nowhere
as a good as the ones in Zagreb or at the
Croatian Club. And then, on my balcony,

squashed together (it's so small), looking down on
the traffic, Jaro lighting my cigarette – ah, I made sure
he could see down the front of my dress. Why didn't
he make a move? He's so damn courteous! I wish he'd
loosen up a bit! I can tell he likes me – can't he see
I'm ready for him? Well, it's gonna be really good
when he finally makes his move. Just let it be soon…

Around two I was woken by a truck backfiring, two
loud bangs some blocks away, and then a third. I went
onto my balcony and lit a fag, gazed at the sky, tried to
spot the Southern Cross and failed, blew a few lopsided
smoke rings. Sirens screamed up King Street. Ambos? Cops?
Smoke smudging the sky further up the hill. Fireys then.
I yawned. Just the usual Newtown music. I ditched
my fag and wandered back to bed.

Disco dynamo

From *The Newtown Voice*, Wednesday, 28 June 1978

Disco Dynamo

The Dancing Machine from Las Vegas, currently at
Le Club in the Cross, has been the talk of Sydney.

But that guy has nothing on Newtown's Dancing
Dynamo. Terry Dickson is just eighteen. He looks

like John Travolta and he dances better. He's
laying them in the aisles at local discos. Besides

his good looks and his personality, he is without
doubt one of the finest dancers seen in Sydney

for many a long year and looks like becoming
the absolute heart-throb of every teeny-bopper

on the disco scene. Terry will be appearing again
at Newtown RSL Club every Thursday night, and

this week everyone who attends will receive an
autographed photo of this sensational new star.

Our very own Disco Dynamo will be judging the
Club's Monster Disco this Thursday night. Great

prizes for the best dancers and the most original
moves. Don't miss the One Man Dancing Machine!

Big boys an small fry

Tom

Over a beer at the Courties, Australia Street, Newtown, Friday, 25 August 1978

Was chattin to Insp. Daly the other day –
I talk to Rod just about every week, he's
OK for a cop – an after we'd chewed over
the vice squad's raids on a couple of brothels
an gambling dens *The Voice*'d brought to their
attention, I asked if there was any advance
in the bombin investigation. I've a hunch that
the King Street bombin was a distraction to confuse
the security people tryin to solve the Hilton

Explosion. After all, they blew up the bank but
didn't steal anythin. Same with the jeweller's.
An who'd blow up a bloody florist? Gotta be
a ruse. Told him I know where there's a coupla
Ananda Marga operatives livin in Queen Street. He
wasn't impressed. Said they were small fry,
all piss an wind, an wouldn't know what to do
with a bomb if they fell over it. Said the King
Street one was a professional job – they found

Two five-gallon plastic containers, a multi-
coloured blanket an a piece of tarp in
the debris – definitely petrol bombs.
The cops haven't tracked down the driver
yet of the yellow Falcon speedin down King
Street straight after the blast. Since they haven't
got any leads, Rod reckons it's an organised
crime job – one scum mob payin' out another.
Small fry, eh? I reckon what Harry and I saw

The other week down South King Street wasn't even
small fry, just a bit a burley on the oily water.
Nice to see our investigative work (the Ed an me)
got another scalp – Marrickville Council's ordered
Harry Kospetas out of his gamblin club in Enmore
Road. We broke the story last week that he had poker
machines in his 'coffee club' upstairs. But he's not
the only one. There's plenty like him, and some
are bigger. The Ed had a good go in his rant (sorry,

Comment) about widespread illegal gamblin, and
the 'big boys' who won't stop at bombin or even
murder. 'Root out the crims,' he thundered. But he
made a good point about the people we saw at that
milkbar. 'For many Greeks and Yugoslavs, gambling
is as natural as two-up and beer is to an Aussie.
Because of the insane nature of Australian gambling
laws, decent people are being turned into criminals.'
He reckons we should make gamblin and brothels legal,
so there's no room for the big boys an their bombs.

Dinner with Harry

Jaroslav

At Harry's, King Street, Newtown, Thursday, 16 February 1978

I went to Harry's place, to her little flat over
a shop. A big room with a window
in the roof: her studio. We looked at her
paintings – fierce colours, angry shapes – then
we drank the wine and ate the food –
spaghetti, 'spag bol' she called it – squashed
together at a small table in her 'lounge' room,
and she asked me to tell her more about life
in Croatia. So romantic, she said.

'... And so I come here to find work and leave
all that behind me. But even here, that stupid
enmity is here in Australia. In Melbourne they
are stabbing people, throwing bombs. Then I
work for a time in the bar at the Croatian
Club in Stanmore; I could find no other work.
But here the people were hating the Jugoslavs
and spitting when they talked of them. They had
angry voices about the government in Zagreb;
they argued with each other at the bar and in
the dining room, even on the dance floor. The
beautiful food and the good wine was soured
with their anger, the music silenced. So I leave
that place and go to work with the railway.
I come to Australia to escape all that stupidity,
to leave it behind in the old Europe; I want
to live the good Aussie life of she'll be right.'

...I can't explain to this girl how lost and abandoned I was after Damir's death; how my glorious city with its towers and gardens, cathedrals and museums, and the Sava running through – even all the little bars and cafés – became an empty icy desert. I can't explain to this girl how time spent in the Broken Hill club was a poorly sketched and smudged copy of all the times spent with Damir and Milo and Marco and the others, laughing and singing and arguing.

Even if I had the English words to say all this, this naïve girl, still so innocent despite her inner-city life, cannot understand, with her talk of making a new life. Damir's death has taken my life, and it matters not how I spend the rest of my years. Whatever this existence is in Australia – on the far side of the moon – it is not a new life.

You can take the girl from Tassie…

Harry

The bar in Kent Street, Sydney, Thursday, 9 February 1978

We'd got into the habit, Jaro and me,
of going to our little bar in Kent street
after class each week, below the level
the footpath down steep narrow stairs.
I called it the subterranean bar. Very
small, private, secret. But it had an
espresso machine that made good
strong coffee, and there was wine.
And Jaro was very good company!

I loved hearing about his life when
he first came to Australia, working
in the mines at Kalgoorlie and Broken
Hill, the work hardening his hands,
muscling up his philosopher's frame, his
Aussie workmates teaching him to speak
English 'like you Aussies speak it, not like
I had learned from reading books'. He
said being able to speak 'dinkum, not

Like some wog', helped him get his job
as a guard on the railway, reeling off
the stations as if reciting poetry. Other times
he'd tell wonderful tales about his life
in Croatia with his friends, fellow students.
It sounded like a dream, the long proud
history, the beautiful buildings, the parks,
the parties, the picnics, the wide river
(he said it sang), and then the horror

The politics and the grief of his friend's
cruel death. That's why he came so far
from his beloved country
to start life all over again.

When Jaro was telling me how much
he loved his homeland, I got to
thinking, well, what do I miss about
the home I left behind – Tasmania?
If I'm honest, no matter how desperate
I was to leave it and relieved to start
afresh here in Sydney, there are things
I miss, tug at my heart if I let them.
Not the parochialism, the insularity, the

Sense of being constantly observed: are
you doing the right thing, behaving your
self, or breaking the unwritten rules? Not
the gossip. The city fathers who are also
people's fathers, uncles, husbands, sons.
The political dynasties, the hidden, secret-
ly acknowledged corruption. None of that!
But I do miss the light. That cool light.
Sydney's sun seems higher in the sky and

Fiercer. The mountains always on the edge
of your vision. Not high, dramatic mountains,
but comforting, familiar, always there, soft
mauvy-blue in the distance, turning indigo
at dusk. I miss the trees – ancient oaks
and elms changing in autumn to russets,
golds and browns, standing brave and bare
in the grey winter light. The damp cool rain
forest olive green, smoky-grey, black

Wood, sassafras, myrtle, dogwood. Man
ferns like overgrown green pineapples tall
around the creeks and waterfalls. Grey
green casuarinas trembling on the
the Gorge's ancient bluestone cliffs.
The Cataract Gorge. My Gorge. So
many moods and faces. A picnic
among aged exotic trees and lawns,
raucous with peacocks and children.
A vigorous walk across the swinging

Bridge, up steep tracks, vertiginous
steps cut into granite faces to look-
outs high above the river, once a
rushing torrent, now a lethargic trickle,
tamed for hydro power. Until winter
rains bring the North Esk tumbling
down the cascades of its gorge in a fury
of cappuccino water, smoke white mist
pouring swirling into mouths, eyes, hair,

Exhilarating, terrifying, tasting its unleashed power. Quiet paths, too; winding unwalked to boulder ledges verandaing silent pools. Shadowed by a fragrant eucalypt, observed only by a magpie and passing blue tongues and skinks, I would sit for hours, sketching and dreaming and occasionally praying.

In Hollis Park

Jaroslav

Hollis Park, Newtown, the night of Thursday, 16 February 1978

I went to the little park at the end of the street, the street with all those grand old houses, the park with those big old trees domed like umbrellas. In the dark beyond the streetlights they could be pillars of San Marco's. I went to the toilet block on Wilson Street to meet someone. I've done it before. On the other side of a door I met someone. No names, no pack drill, he whispered. It was quick but it was relief. The next someone came much slower. Didn't speak. I muttered a greeting he didn't understand. No names, no pack drill, whispered the third one – someone else. I'd hoped someone would come back to me. Walking back through the park. Suddenly. The sky. Smashed open. With light. The thump. Came after. I'm flat to the earth, clutching grass. The thump bucks my stomach. Chest. Eyes squeezed tight. Not to see what I'd seen already. The building split open, flames running and jumping, broken-backed books spurting out, burning paper whirling ashy-leaved on people – bloodied shattered people. Damir lying at my feet. Stood up. Dodged. Ran whimpering. Choked on bile and oily smoke. Hid behind a pillar. Green blood smeared across my face and hands. The moon comes out. I see trees houses the footpath my hands my trousers. How long was I…? I stink of shit and fear. I hear the screaming of sirens tearing up King Street.

I nearly got arrested

Buzz

At Harry's, King Street, Newtown, Sunday, 25 June 1978

God, Harry, I had a close shave yesterday! Coulda
got myself arrested. Wouldn't a done me any good,
what with squattin' illegally (yeah, yeah, I know, all
squattin's illegal, smart-arse), bein picked as a lesbian

I'd lose my job at the garage an WEA wouldn't
want me teachin car maintenance any more, either.
See, I went to the International Gay Solidarity Day
in Hyde Park yesterday. Put on by the local Gay

Solidarity Group – some of the girls I'm pally with at
the Tin Sheds – some of the guys too, they're members
of this group – so I said I'd go along to show solidarity
too. It was interestin stuff, talks about what life's like

for homosexuals – gays AN lesbians, after Stonewall,
in the US an in England, where they've got that Festival
of Light shit run by Mrs Mary Whitehouse. The old bat's
comin here in a coupla weeks to speak at a national

Conference on homosexuality, an she wants to tell us
how wrong an evil we are, an how we wanta destroy
society. It was a beaut day, mostly lesbians an gays
but some straights too, showin solidarity with us.

By 4 p.m. I'd had enough solidarity, an headed back to the squat. Some of the girls said Aren't ya comin to tonight's march, but I said Nah, got the early mornin shift at Crispy Hot bakery. So I missed

All the drama. Read about it in the *Sun* between servin customers. Two thousand people, the *Sun* reckoned, marchin an singin along Oxford street at 11 p.m., past all the bars and clubs. The cops

Corralled em all in Darlo Road that they'd closed off an got stuck into them with batons an boots (readin between the lines). They arrested 53 people, who're in the cells now waitin to go to

Court. I coulda got caught too, if I'd gone with the girls. Life's tough when you're not straight.

Dempsey Family wins

From *The Newtown Voice*, Wednesday, 23 August 1978

Dempsey Family Wins 3-Year Battle Against Council

The Dempsey family has won its battle against South Sydney Council to convert a deserted factory into

a large communal house. In 1975, ten people decided to buy the empty Dempsey & Co. factory in Shepherd

Street, Darlington, and convert it into a house. It had been empty since 1972 and was in an area zoned for single

family dwellings. In 1975, the Family approached Council seeking formal approval to change the factory's use. But

Council said the Dempsey Family was not a real family, quoting local government ordinances giving it power

to refuse people who were not immediate family to live under the same roof. The Family pointed out that nearly

one-third of the population – students, migrants, people in de facto relationships, and Aborigines – lived together

although unrelated. In March, the Family lodged its building application to Council for approval to buy and occupy

the factory. After three rejections Council's building department finally passed it. But the Council wouldn't approve

The plans. For the third time the Family took its case to the Local Government Appeals Tribunal, and late last week was granted the necessary approval. The Dempsey Family representative, Mr Colin James, said that in the past five

years, ten thousand people had been forced out of the city by commercial expansion and the building of expressways.

(He did not mention Sydney University's relentless growth which has caused the demolition of many family homes.)

'We are concerned about bringing people back to the City,' he said, 'and while there are few large houses suitable for

communal living in South Sydney, there is no shortage of vacant factories which could be cheaply converted. Apart

from students,' he said, he thought there would be 'many people who would like the chance to live communally.'

Cathy's Child

Harry

Albermarle Street and Australia Street, Newtown, Monday, 19 June 1978

Buzz woke me up early this morning, throwing
two cent coins at my window. Quick, get dressed
an come down, we're gonna watch the filming. Err,
what? I mumbled, not fully awake. The filming,
she said, impatiently, *Cathy's Child*, come on, we
gotta get a good pozzie. We scooted round to
the Carlisle Castle, a couple of blocks from the

Courthouse (both the real court next to the cop
shop, and the pub. Newie's got a pub on every
corner, just about). There was already a bit of
a crowd hanging round when we got there, a whiff
of excitement on the dope and ciggy smoke.
Seems the director and film crew like Newie's
'ethnic atmosphere', according to the paper,

And some scenes were going to be filmed in
the Carlisle. Handy too for shots of the cop shop
as well as locals pretending to be going about
their usual business. We spotted Tom with his
tape recorder and notebook, talking to someone
important – maybe the director – so we waved,
and he ignored us. There's some big names

Involved in this film, apart from the lead, who
we'd never heard of. Apparently it's her first
big role. Then the 'minders' rounded us all up
and shoved us behind ropes, and the cameras
rolled down the street and the action began. It
was exciting, but too short, just a couple of bits
of dialogue in the street between the guy playing

The reporter and the girl playing Cathy, which
they had to do a few times until the director
was happy. Then they went into the pub with
the cameras following, but we weren't allowed
to go inside to watch. The minders were stern
and very beefy. Buzz reckoned they'd make good
nightclub bouncers. Tom was still hanging around,

So we bounced up to him and Buzz suggested we
go to the Courties, even though it was only 10 a.m.
I don't usually drink before midday and I was really
hungry, but the Courties had it sorted with a mean
egg and bacon roll. Apparently it's a known hang
over cure and they make them every morning. Tom
told us some funny yarns about the cops and local

Identities, maybe a bit slanderous, but I don't
know any of the people he was gossiping about,
so it didn't matter. Buzz was cackling away; being
a local, she knew just who Tom was talking about.
It was fun, the three of us, beers and bacon rolls
and a lazy winter's morning in Newie.

Latchkey kids

Front page of *The Newtown Voice*, Wednesday, 20 September 1978

LATCHKEY KIDS OUT ON STREET
Welfare services slashed

Latchkey kids in Newtown and Marrickville will be thrown out into the street because of Federal Government delays and

cuts in funding. A church running welfare activities for latchkey kids will have to cut back savagely on its services. For

months, the Marrickville Baptist Church has been running into debt to keep its services going. It has been waiting on an

answer about funds from the Minister for Social Security, (Sen. Guilfoyle), since the end of May. Last week the crisis

got so bad that the church threatened to go to the Federal Ombudsman to get some action. On that same day, it got

unofficial word that it wasn't going to get the $50,000 it had asked for. The church is now slashing its program to pieces.

After-school activities for 40 latchkey kids will go by the board. Holiday programs for 200 children will be dropped.

Latchkey kids are children whose parents are at work all day. Many come from one parent families. Often they have house

keys on a string around their neck so they can let themselves into their empty homes after school. Some children were also

turning up at school not long after seven. They had been given money to buy a packet of chips for breakfast. (As described in our front-page story on 21 June, St Peter's school has applied to the Education Department to provide

milkshakes for undernourished children, and Darlington School had previously applied for funds to supply breakfast

to such children, but neither of them has received funding.) The church began operating an after-school and holiday

program in 1975 to cater for latchkey children. Nearly all of its funds have come from government sources, including the

now-dead Australian Assistance Plan. Meanwhile the church's small congregation has made massive efforts through its

generous volunteers to keep the service going and keep it cheap. However, the church says there is no way that it can

operate without funding as demand for these services has mushroomed because of the area's pressing social needs.

Routine

Jaroslav
Hordern Street, Newtown, April 1978

I go to work, I come home, I drink my coffee out on the back step. I go to bed, I sleep, I dream. I wake up, shivering and sweating.

I go to work; sometimes I go to the little bar and drink the wine with the barman, and smoke, and make small conversation. I go home and dream and wake up, shivering and sweating.

I go to work; sometimes I go to the little bar and drink the wine with the barman, and smoke, and make small conversation. Then I go to Hyde Park. I do not again go to the toilet block in Hollis Park.

When I go to Hyde Park, always the pretty Turkish boy begs me to take him home with me. Always I refuse. There is not room for him and the dream that wakes me every night, sweating and shivering.

Illegal clubs in full swing

From *The Newtown Voice*, Wednesday, 13 September 1978

Illegal clubs in full swing

Inspector Neil Young of the Vice Squad has categorically refused to meet with or talk to the President of Newtown

Chamber of Commerce under any circumstances, the president, Dr J. Meissner claimed at the weekend.

Dr Meissner made the claim in an interview with *The Voice* after a surprise visit to the gambling clubs around Newtown

and Marrickville. His tour was made during the Saturday afternoon 'peak' SP period. He visited all the major clubs

in King Street, Enmore Road and Marrickville Road. Dr Meissner said he was 'astounded' at the brazen nature

of their operations and the ease with which he had gained entry to most of them. 'Obviously these clubs must have

protection if they are operating so openly and close to local police stations,' he said. Most clubs had poker machines,

although the one at 159 Enmore Road no longer had any. A club at 23A King Street had three poker machines, two bingos,

but no SP betting. 'A club at 324A King Street had poker machines, bingos and SP betting all in full swing, with

the "odds" supplied from a central office over a loudspeaker.' For the first time in his life, he had been thrown out of a club, because the manager said 'you're not a member'. At 159 Enmore Road, which has been served with a notice to close

by Marrickville Council, he saw 50 or 60 people on the premises, SP betting sheets on display and loudspeakers

blaring. Dr Meissner said he failed to gain entrance to another club at 281 Marrickville Road when a burly doorman

descended from the second floor and politely informed him 'Full up, mate. No room.' Dr Meissner said the sound of

numerous poker machines being played was audible from the entrance. He would discuss the clubs' operations with fellow

Chamber of Commerce members, he said, and also raise it with Marrickville Council. It was not fair that police should

regularly raid the smaller clubs and leave the larger clubs untouched for years. Asked to expand on his statement

about Insp. Young, Dr Meissner said he had been trying to arrange a meeting with the police and the Chamber about

the spread of vice in the Newtown area. The inspector had categorically refused to meet 'in no uncertain terms'.

At the disco

Harry

Newtown RSL, Enmore Road. Newtown, Saturday, 1 July 1978

On Saturday night Tom and I went
to the disco at the RSL – 'the Rissole',
he calls it, though I'm sure he gives
it a ruder name. We went to see New
town's 'Dancing Dynamo', Terry Dixon,
who's supposed to be better than John
Travolta, even, showing off his new

Moves. There were comps too for people
who fancied themselves disco devils. I
wore Buzz's white flares, which I'd taken
to the laundrette with my stuff, a stripy
crop top and my boots – getting shabby
but with a nice high heel. We had a beaut
time. Tom's a great dancer with a real feel

For the music, and I was really getting off
on the beats. It was huge fun. We came
second in one of the comps. In the break,
while the Dynamo was strutting his stuff,
Tom brought me a beer and some salted
peanuts. We make good team, you an me,
plonking them down and sitting close. Bet

Your middle-aged boyfriend can't dance like
me. He's not my boyfriend! (I wish…) Well, I
dunno what you see in him. I mean, he's not
a real man, he's just a sad old poofta. No, I
said, you've got it wrong. He's cultured, so-
phisticated, European. He's a gentleman. You
don't understand. Just because he's not ocker

Like you and your mates, he's not, he's not a
homosexual! Yes he is, said Tom. He's a fag,
an you're too blind to see it. Sophisticated, my
foot! Degenerate's more like it. You're kiddin
yourself if you can't see that. Open your bloody
eyes, Harry! I pushed my chair back, stood up,
mumbled sorry, I feel sick, gotta go home. I was

Shaky, trying not to cry. Why hadn't I realised? Why
was I so stupid? After David's death I should have
been more aware. Jaro's grieving for Damir made
perfect sense. Tom offered to drive me, but I could-
n't bear to sit beside him. He walked me to the door
and watched me stumble off. Out of sight, I tugged
off my boots and ran barefoot all the way home.

The Greek conspiracy

Tom

Over a beer at the Courties, Australia Street, Friday, 1 December 1978

Startin to think this whole multiculturalism business
isn't as easy as politicians'd have us believe – like
rememberin not to call em wogs an dagos any more,
an gettin our tongues around their names, an the names
of their food, even the good stuff like souvlaki an tzatziki.
Are we still even allowed to call em New Australians? Any
how, I reckon it's pretty tough on the migrants too. Take

This whole Greek Conspiracy shemozzle, aka the Medicare
Fraud. When the story broke in the *Herald* back in April,
it was big news, an we followed it a bit in the *Voice*. In dawn
raids, the Commonwealth cops entered 160 homes and five
doctors' surgeries an arrested 181 Greek pensioners, most
of em in Marrickville, Dulwich Hill, Petersham, Stanmore an
Newie, an chucked em in the cells on $1,000 bail. Some of em

Were in the lock-up for days until their rellies or welfare groups
could scrape up the dosh. One poor woman was attacked in her
cell by a druggie comin down from a high. They were charged
with conspirin with dodgy Greek doctors to defraud Medicare
by claimin disability payments an invalid pensions for back
pain. It was spread all over the *Herald*'s front page, an
the *Sun*, too. The reporters'd been invited beforehand by

The cops to make a good story. Which it was. Specially since, as well as the hundreds, maybe thousands of 'pay cheats' in the country, there was supposed to be hundreds more in Greece 'livin in luxury' on Aussie invalid pensions. The Feds were watchin all the airports to stop any other 'fraudulent Greeks' leavin the country. Nearly 700 people on Social Security had their benefits taken away and their

Payments stopped without any warnin. Not a good time to be a Greek, specially a pensioner! Well that was eight months ago, an now it's nearly Christmas. The welfare agencies – Greek an Aussie in Redfern and Marrickville – have been fightin for these poor people all this time, an are demanding the charges be dropped an the victims paid compo. Dunno if that'll ever happen, but good on em for tryin.

Specially when so many of the poor buggers're struggling to live, pay rent, buy groceries. Back when the whole hoo-ha blew up, 181 people were taken to court, but only four were found guilty of defrauding the Commonwealth. Three of em even pleaded guilty. But the government is still houndin the others. A few of them have actually dropped dead or killed themselves from the stress. An there's plenty who dunno how they're gonna buy Christmas presents for their kiddies. Seems like they haven't had a fair go.

Blacks not wanted

Front page of *The Newtown Voice*, Wednesday, 6 September 1978

RACISM IN HOUSING
BLACKS NOT WANTED

It seems some Newtown real estate agents are refusing to rent homes to Aboriginal families on racial grounds. They are

forced to take second-rate housing at rip-off rents. Several cases have been referred to the State counsellor on equal

opportunity. However, it's hard to pin down cases of overt discrimination. In some cases tests have been made by

South Sydney Community Aid. Black families have been told specific houses were not available, but when a white person

visited the agents the same houses were available. Robert Mowbray of South Sydney Community Aid said racism was

'rampant' among some estate agents. The problem had got worse in recent months, he said, because of the current

'grave shortage' in rental accommodation, which made it very difficult for people to get land or housing without a

long search. 'On top of this, Aboriginal people face marked discrimination by some estate agents and landlords,' Mr

Mowbray said. This was despite the fact that it was illegal under both Federal and State laws. In recent weeks South

Sydney Community Aid has dealt with many complaints from Aboriginal families over discrimination. 'It appears they have been rejected for accommodation on racial grounds.' Last week, the centre's welfare officer, Ms Brenda Marks, was involved in two such cases. In one, a young Aboriginal woman had gone to an estate agent in Newtown, wanting to rent a house she knew was vacant. The agent asked for references and she produced an excellent reference from another agent. She was then told the owner would not rent the house to her. No reason was given. The other case concerned a young couple with a child. They tried several agents around Newtown, hoping to rent a two-bedroom house. Three agents refused to show them any houses, yet when Ms Marks asked about the same houses they were available. She finally found a place for the family to rent, but it had only one bedroom and was quite expensive for its size.

After the disco

Tom

Newtown RSL, Enmore Road, Newtown, Thursday, 6 July 1978

Seems Harry was pretty upset, rushin
off like that after I told her her 'boyfriend',
(he's gotta be over 40), is a fag. He's too
old for a fairy or a nancy boy, so he is what
I said – a sad old poofta. Dunno why she'd
want to go round with a fag. Bad enough
she's friends with that whacko lezzo. But
I really like Harry (though I don't much

Like her stupid name). She's pretty, she's
a great dancer, looks good in jeans as well
as a tight dress, an she likes me. We had
a ripper time tonight – until I went an
opened my big mouth an put my bloody
foot in it! So what am I gonna do? Maybe
she'll calm down, come round to my way
of thinkin. Specially if I sweet talk her a bit.

Buy her somethin nice. Maybe flowers? We
got on famously at the Carlisle the other day
after the film shoot. Beaut way to spend a
mornin, in the pub with a beer an a bird ya
fancy. We make a real good-lookin couple.
Her an me in the Falcon, yeah… Christ, I
dunno. She's the first bird I've really been
serious about, an I've bloody fucked it up.

Life wasn't meant to be easy

Buzz

At Harry's, King Street, Newtown, Saturday, 28 October 1978

Jeez, Harry, when Malcolm Fraser told us
life wasn't meant to be easy – the smug
patronisin bastard – I didn't think it was
gunna get this bloody tough! I don't

Mean for me – I'm OK, snug in my
squat, an I have some work. It's people
like the old folk bein' evicted by the uni
an forced to live in a grotty shack with

A dunny down the yard, in a street where
they don't know anyone. What if they fall
over, need help? Who're they gunna ask?
Then there's others tossed out by Housing

Cos they're a bit rowdy or got a drug habit,
or their dad beats them or molests them
or they're a bit schizo. There's single mums
can't find a safe place, an ordinary people

Strugglin to pay bills livin in shit cos greedy
landlords put the rent up. Didya know, now
the uni's so big, rents've gone up by a third
in twelve months? I read it in *The Voice*, so

It's dinkum. It's the demand for student
housin. Students sharin a house, four
or five together can pay more than
a family or a single mum can afford.

The kids get the better houses, an the
landlords turf out people who can't pay
higher rents, so they have to settle for
shit places, or queue up for emergency

Housin. Seems like things are almost as
bad as in the Depression, specially in
Newie an Marrickville. Welfare groups say
lotsa people are sleepin in parks an cars.

An guess what? Accordin to *The Voice*
there's plenty of places empty that are
owned by the government – blocksa flats
for migrants in Marrickville and Annandale,

But never been used. Jeez, Harry, I dunno,
where's this country goin? What happened
to the lucky country? To a fair go for every
one? I reckon we need a bloody revolution!
An I mean Bloody!

What Tom Doesn't Know

What Tom doesn't know,
what his investigative
journalist's nose
hasn't sussed out,
is that Tom is
part-Aboriginal.

What Tom's father
Patrick doesn't know
is that his mother
was raped
by the white man
she cleaned for
and whose children
she cared for.

What Tom and his
father Patrick
don't know
is that Nellie
(Tom's grandmother)
was also half-caste,
Nellie's mother
used for recreation
by the Irish
station owner
in whose kitchen
she worked.

Tom and his father
know nothing
of their family's past.
Patrick
was adopted
from an orphanage
when he was
three years old.

Fighting the Yowie

Front page of *The Newtown Voice*, Wednesday, 1 November 1978

RESIDENTS FIGHT AS UNI EXPANDS
Elderly people living in fear

Darlington residents who resent Sydney University's destruction of their community are starting to fight back.

People are not going to be pushed out of their homes without a fight, and 80 have signed a petition to South Sydney

Council. The petition objects to further redevelopment in what is left of Darlington. Council has deferred a decision on

the proposed development in nine acres bounded by Darlington Road, Golden Grove, Abercrombie and Darlington streets.

The university owns most of the land, and year after year has uprooted residents since it grew too big for its City Road

site. Ald. Beverley Hunter, who presented the petition to Council, said she doubted it would do any good. 'There's no

stopping them, but if you don't try you don't get anywhere.' She said a welfare worker has advised some residents of

their right not to leave unless they are evicted. 'The university wants them out of their homes to make way for

more development. If some people stick up for themselves, others will.' In past years people have moved without putting

the university to the inconvenience of legal proceedings, she said. 'They got frightened into it.' Some have had three or four moves in the past six years. 'It's not good for the elderly people. They're too old to be pushed around.' One pensioner,

forced to leave familiar surroundings, had been offered a house with an outdoor toilet and no fences. 'She would be

frightened to go to the toilet at night. She wouldn't know any neighbours and wouldn't have anyone to help her if she

got sick.' Some elderly people had died shortly after they were relocated, Ald. Hunter said. 'They never settled in.'

The university now wants to demolish the home of a woman, a pensioner, who has lived in the same place for 35 years.

She and the other residents who signed the petition think the university has gone quite far enough, and that any

further development should be in the outer suburbs, not in the university's backyard and people's homes.

Johnny Raper sticks his oar in

Tom

Newtown Leagues Club, Stanmore Road, Enmore, Friday, 29 September 1978

Bloody Johnny Raper! He may be a good
Rugby league player – well, he is Newtown
Jets coach – but sometimes he doesn't know
his arse from his elbow. Monday night,
for example. I was covering the Koori do –
a mayoral reception for the Koories Junior
footy team. There's been a bit of bad blood
here at the club between Newtown supporters

An the Koories, an some club staff seem to
have a down on the Koori players. Koories
say it's racism, an they're alleging people
have been threatened and even bashed, or
thrown out of the club. They've written to
the club secretary an are gonna boycott

The club until they get satisfaction. Anyhow,
the Mayor, Ald. Harrison, makes a big deal
at this shindig of supporting the Koories, an
announced he'd appointed a junior liaison
officer for the Koories on the council. So it's
all over bar the shoutin, when in walks
King Johnny. He immediately gets stuck
into them, and tells them to 'settle down

An be peaceable', that conflict's not good
for either side. When he mentions Newie
club secretary, Frank Farrington, lots of
Koories started booin. He gets on his high
horse then. 'You boo Frank Farrington an
you're booin me. I won't tolerate it.' Then
the idiot says he doesn't know the Koories
very well, but he'd make it his business

To get to know them. Meant to be friendly,
but sure sounded like a threat. To be fair,
he did say he'd watch their performance
so's he could pick players for the seniors.
Anyhow, Koories club officials told me later
they were not impressed with Mr Johnny
Raper or his approach to peace-makin.

Pretty poor, Harry, pretty poor

Harry

King Street, Newtown, the night of Thursday, 6 July 1978

Jaro didn't meet me after WEA tonight.
After what Tom said at the disco on
Saturday night, I've been thinking a lot
about Jaro. I've realised – guiltily –
I haven't seen him
since the night he came to dinner
and I fed him spag bol and frozen cheesecake.

Did I offend him? Was my food so awful,
my conversation so insipid,
that he doesn't want my company any more?
He hasn't met me at WEA since.
I'm feeling guilty, too, that I've been having fun
with Buzz and Tom – going to discos, pubs, Greek
places, just hanging around together –

and I hadn't even thought about Jaro till Tom's
mean comment. What kind of friend does that
make me? Jaro's lonely; I was lonely too,
then I made some friends my own age
and I just forgot about him. What would my dad
say? Pretty poor, Harry, pretty poor. The bank
and those shops further up the street were

bombed that night…surely that has nothing to do with Jaro not seeing me again? He would've been asleep in his bed like the rest of Newtown, have no idea about it till Tom's front-page story. I don't have Jaro's phone number, I don't even know where in Newie he lives. But I'd like to see him again, if only to apologise.

How am I going to find him? I could maybe go to the little bar, ask the barman if he knows Jaro's phone number. Hmm, might not look good. A single woman in a secluded bar by herself. What about the Art Gallery? He used to go there some Sundays. I'll go on Sunday and hope to see him. If not, there's always art!

In the rain

Harry

AGNSW and the Domain, Sydney, Sunday, 9 July 1978

It was raining this morning, so I almost
didn't go to the Art Gallery. I haven't
acclimatised yet to Sydney's weather.
It can rain really heavily – like a
tropical downpour – ten minutes later
you're steaming and sweating.
Not like Tassie's cold rain that chills

You to the bone if you don't rug up. And
those thunderstorms! They come
out of nowhere
in the middle of the day,
flashing and crackling and booming.
Terrifying! I used to love lying awake
at night listening to the thunder rolling

Around the hills cradling the valley,
round and round, and me snug and safe
in bed. So it took an effort to walk out
my door and catch a bus to Hyde Park.
Taking the shortcut to AGNSW from behind
the Eye Hospital, I wondered if Jaro had
taken the same route, and was sheltering

Inside. But he wasn't there.
Not in any of the rooms, empty
apart from a few elderly tourists and a
bored security guard. The kiosk under
the fig trees across the way?
Not there. Where then? Where?
The rain had stopped, but the clouds

Hung raggedly, as if unsure
whether to stay or go. But I had to find him;
it felt like life or death. And there,
further into the Domain than I'd been before,
there he was, sitting calmly on a rockshelf
sheltered by a tall gum, smoking, gazing
at the grey water and the grey ships

Berthed at Woolloomooloo. His hair was wet, and
his jacket, but he sat unmoving, until I
broke his calm. We walked back to the gallery,
and I told him the truth about David.

Pushing Rod into the drink

Harry

Launceston, Tasmania, 24 February 1976

After I pushed Rod into the river
he told me the truth about David
and him – his role in it all, the
bastard! Not forgetting that sleaze
Toby, but it's Rod I blame. It's him
I can't forgive. Of course I didn't
mean to push him in the river. It
was just a happy accident. It was
inevitable that we'd drift apart ex-
cept we didn't drift. I shoved! We

were more than a little pissed – too
many daiquiris on the *Sylvania*'s
deck on a Sunday arvo showing
off to a federal politician. (Rod had
big-fish little-pond ambitions.) His
arm around my shoulders propriet-
orially. My beautiful wife thinks
she's an artist. You ever hear the
likes of that Mal? An aaartist! I am
an artist, I yelled, forgetting my

role as the would-be politician's
gorgeous complaisant spouse. I
turned, facing him, jabbed my
fingers hard against his chest. I
am an artist and a bloody good
one! Trust Rod to lose his balance.
He stumbled over the rail and tumbled into the Tamar's toxic water!
The truth about David had been
hinted at but never spoken aloud

Till Rod put it into vicious words
I'd no choice but to hear, thrown
in my face, words toxic as the water
he'd splashed into. It's an old story.
Nothing new in Tassie's hypocrisy.
Toby was gay and so was my kid
brother. Toby seduced David in
their final year. To hide the crime
that sleaze persuaded Rod – best
friends since prep school – to hang

around with them, just three guys
together, out for drinks and fun.
Even in year eleven Rod was known
for drinking and driving (his dad's
yellow Merc) and picking up girls,
taking them to bed on the back seat.
That threesome was perfect cover
for the 'filthy perverted activities' Rod
accused David of involving Toby in.
Bored with David, Toby left for

Melbourne's brighter lights and bigger
opportunities. 'Your brother was a
piece of worthless shit,' Rod snarled.
'He was bloody useless. All he had to do
was keep his head down and his nose
clean and Toby's people and my father
would've seen to it that nothing ever
came out. The stupid git didn't have
to go and hang himself.'

David and Damir

Jaroslav

Hordern Street, Newtown, Sunday evening, 9 July 1978

Harry is a strange girl. And yet, I like her. When she found me on the Domain today, she seemed agitated, distressed, and kept apologising – for what? Some fault she thought she had made, something she had done to drive me away. It took some minutes to calm her down. Then she told me about her brother.

In reply, I pulled out the photo of Damir that has nestled against my heart for these so long years. It is crumpled at the edges, warm from my blood. I told her we were lovers. And then I told her about the night in Hollis Park.

So now we both know. There are not any more, secrets between us.

Back at the Salona Bistro

From *The Newtown Voice*, Wednesday, 15 November 1978

Bistro beaten in court battle
Win for residents

Hollis Park residents are jubilant over a court victory over the Salona bistro in Georgina Street. Last week the Salona

had its cabaret licence cancelled by the Licensing Court. It is the latest phase in a long-term battle residents and South

Sydney Council have been having with the Salona. They have even formed a residents' development committee to fight this

and other issues, such as the massage parlour in nearby Fitzroy Street. The bistro had a cabaret licence to operate

to three a.m., but residents say it often remains open until four or five. They have complained repeatedly about the loud

music, and the noise people make as they leave at closing time. They say there are arguments and fights, and people

have urinated in the street. Despite recent approaches to the management, nothing had been done. 'Every weekend

it's like a bombing raid,' one resident said. 'You can't get any sleep and your health begins to suffer.' Finally, they decided

to fight against the renewal of the cabaret licence. Forty affidavits were prepared and thirteen residents gave evidence

in the Licensing Court. South Sydney Council has been helping the residents, providing a lawyer to help them fight the case.

Last week, the licensing magistrate ruled that the grounds
of the objection had been admitted, and cancelled

the restaurant's cabaret licence. The Salona must now close
at midnight. The next day, South Sydney Council ordered

the large neon sign above the bistro entrance on Georgina
Street be taken down. The Salona's management have

reattached the sign across the restaurant's King Street
frontage, where it's brightly lit at night.

www.ingramcontent.com/pod-product-compliance
Lightning Source LLC
Chambersburg PA
CBHW070922080526
44589CB00013B/1398